贝贝熊系列丛书
The Berenstain Bears

AF709048

AND TOO MUCH PRESSURE

找回轻松

当孩子们，还有他们的家长们，都有点儿忙过头了的时候，他们的生活就会变得有些混乱。

第一时间的启蒙书

贝贝熊系列丛书
The Berenstain Bears

AND TOO MUCH PRESSURE
我回轻松

(美) 斯坦·博丹　简·博丹　绘著
Stan & Jan Berenstain
孙志芳等　译

父母和孩子一起阅读
家长和子女共同成长

新疆青少年出版社

如果有人问起谁是熊王国里最忙碌的，也许你会说是蜜蜂。因为他们整天忙着采集花粉，酿制蜂蜜，保护蜂巢，还要做所有为他们赢得“勤劳的蜜蜂”这一称号的事。

也许你会说水獭是最忙的。他们砍伐树木、修建水坝、搭造带秘密水下入口的小屋。毫无疑问，水獭确实很忙。

但是如果你的回答真是蜜蜂或者水獭，那就错了。因为，最近熊王国里最忙的，莫过于我们的朋友贝贝熊一家了。

贝贝熊一家并不总是这么忙。以前，他们做的事情跟其他家庭没什么两样：他们工作、玩耍、去上学、拜访朋友、享受大自然——有时候，他们只是坐在一起，什么也不做。

贝贝熊一家也没计划要忙成这样，但事情好像悄悄地跟在了他们身后——

先是小熊哥哥和棒球联盟的事；

然后是小熊妹妹，因为对芭蕾舞着迷，她开始上芭蕾课；

当小熊妹妹最好的朋友丽兹开始上骑马课的时候，她也想去参加了——而小熊哥哥当然也不可能被落在一旁，尤其是遇到骑马这种好玩的事情。

其他活动也是这样开始的——只要他们的某个朋友参加了什么，小熊哥哥和小熊妹妹也都要参加。大家还没来得及说声“足够了”，他们就已经报了名……

空手道

美术

还有计算机俱乐部

说起忙，熊妈妈或者熊爸爸必须每天开车送小熊兄妹去参加所有这些活动。

事情变得超级复杂，熊妈妈不得不做了一张大大的时间表，才能知道下一步该干什么。熊爸爸把时间表挂在墙上。

星期五的事情尤其多——而今天就是星期五。

“谁去接一下电话？”电话响了四声以后，熊妈妈喊道，“我正忙着把今天晚上要做的菜从冰箱里拿出来呢。”

“现在不行！”小熊妹妹从楼上喊道，“我正换衣服准备上芭蕾课呢！”

“我也不行！”小熊哥哥叫道，“我正在穿棒球服呢！”

而熊爸爸正在外面修车，熊妈妈只好自己去接电话了。在响第七下的时候，她拿起了话筒。熊奶奶似乎已经在电话那头等了很久。

“你好？”熊妈妈说。

“你好，亲爱的。”熊奶奶说，“都还好吧？你听起来有点儿气喘吁吁的。”

“有点儿，”熊妈妈说，“我刚才在厨房，正从冰箱里拿东西。孩子们在楼上准备去学芭蕾和打棒球，熊爸爸——”

她刚要解释熊爸爸的事，肩上的挎包不小心挂住了电话线，电话被拽到了地上，发出“哐当”一声响。

“怎么了？”奶奶喊道，“这么大一声响！”

“只不过是电话掉了——有什么事情吗，奶奶？”熊妈妈没想到，当她弯腰去捡电话的时候，她的帽子也掉了，而当她想去捡帽子的时候，她又绊住了电话线，重重地摔坐在地板上。

“我就是想请你们一家最近过来一起吃晚饭。”熊奶奶说。

“我很想去，奶奶，但是我们马上要出门了，所以等我回头看看时间表，再给您回电话好吗？”

“好的，”奶奶顿了顿，说，“好吧，再见亲爱的。”

“妈妈！”小熊妹妹吃惊地说，“你坐在地上玩电话线干吗？快点儿，我们要迟到了！”

“先送我去！”小熊哥哥一边往车那边走，一边喊。

“不行，先送我！”小熊妹妹也喊。

“不行，先送我！”小熊哥哥坚持着。

当熊爸爸想解释一下车子有问题——需要清理火花塞的时候——熊妈妈大喊："现在没时间，亲爱的！"就开车走了，留给熊爸爸一身尘土。

"嗯，"熊奶奶挂上电话，说，"很明显，树屋里有不少事情要做。"

"年轻人就是那样，"熊爷爷说，"他们喜欢出去做些事情。想当初，我还年轻的时候——"

“做是一回事，”熊奶奶说，“可是做过头，”她叹气道，“却是另外一回事了。”

如果熊爸爸听到了熊奶奶的这番话，他肯定会同意。他们有太多事情要做了——太多来来往往，太多匆匆忙忙，太大压力。贝贝熊一家的时间表已经成了一个恶梦——事实证明，那确实成了一连串恶梦。

小熊兄妹本来打算晚上看看电视，可是他们累极了，身子都僵硬了——小熊妹妹刚上完芭蕾课，小熊哥哥刚打完棒球——他们早早就上了床，睡着了，并且做了一整晚梦。

　　小熊妹妹梦见她上了一个奇怪的旋转木马——这个旋转木马上都是她的课外活动，转啊转啊转。她想下来，但是不管她怎么努力，就是下不来。

　　小熊哥哥也做了个梦。他梦见自己被卷进了一阵巨大的龙卷风里，到处都是棒球、足球，还有计算机。

熊爸爸梦见他被困在了一张魔毯上，向一个黑洞飞去。实际上那不是魔毯，而是墙上那张可恶的时间表。

熊妈妈没做恶梦，因为她一夜都没睡着。她就那么一直醒着，盯着黑漆漆的房间，想着怎样才能熬过明天。

三口两口吃过早饭后，熊妈妈给熊爸爸准备好了午餐，这时他已经去森林里工作了。紧接着，熊妈妈催孩子们上车："快点儿！"她说，"今天会很忙。有美术课、足球班、空手道，还有游泳课，然后我们还得挤出时间吃午饭和买东西。"

他们上了车，熊妈妈转动钥匙，可是引擎发动不起来。她又试了一次，车还是不能启动。

“快点儿，妈妈！”小熊哥哥嚷道，“我们的空手道老师对迟到的处罚很严厉。”

“足球教练更严！”小熊妹妹叫道。

熊妈妈试了一次又一次。

“快点儿，妈妈！”他俩一起嚷起来，在座位上又蹦又跳。但是不管熊妈妈怎么努力，车子还是纹丝不动。

接着，熊妈妈做了一件孩子们从来也没有见过的事：她哭了起来。大颗大颗的眼泪从她的面颊上流了下来。孩子们顿时忘了空手道、足球和其他所有的事，他们只知道，他们的妈妈哭了。

“怎么了？”小熊哥哥问。

“告诉我们吧，求你了！”小熊妹妹说。但熊妈妈只是哭着走上台阶，进了屋。

“快去找爸爸！”小熊妹妹对哥哥说，“我去陪妈妈。”

小熊妹妹跟着熊妈妈进了她的房间，熊妈妈倒在床上不停地流泪。小熊妹妹唯一能做的，就是不让自己也哭出来。

“妈妈出事了！你得快回去！”小熊哥哥在森林里找到了正在工作的熊爸爸，告诉了他发生的事。熊爸爸发觉到小熊哥哥对熊妈妈哭了这件事很失望。

“儿子，谁都会有哭的时候。”熊爸爸说。

“连你也会？”小熊哥哥问。

“有时候，”熊爸爸说，“车的问题出在火花塞上，我们可能得换新的了。但是真正的问题是咱们的时间表。我知道昨晚妈妈一直没睡好，在担心那些事情。”

“我也没睡好，我做了恶梦。”小熊哥哥赞同道。

“那就是说我们两个都做恶梦了。”熊爸爸说。

“妹妹也做了恶梦。”小熊哥哥说，这时候他们已经快到树屋了。

“妈妈已经不哭了！”熊爸爸和小熊哥哥上楼时，小熊妹妹宣布说。

“是的，”熊妈妈微笑着说，脸上还挂着几颗泪珠，“有时候，没有什么比大哭一场更痛快的了。”

“最好还是学会一些应付压力的方法。”熊爸爸说。

于是，贝贝熊一家立刻就地召开了家庭会议。孩子们同意每周只参加两种课外活动，这样就足够了。小熊哥哥选了棒球和计算机俱乐部，小熊妹妹选了芭蕾和骑马。

的确——他们失去了“熊王国最忙碌的一家”的头衔。但是他们回到了正常的生活，重新开始做和其他家庭一样的事。他们工作、玩耍、去上学、拜访朋友、享受大自然——

有时候，他们只是坐在一起，什么也不做。

The Berenstain Bears

AND TOO MUCH PRESSURE

When cubs and their parents get a little too busy,
their everyday lives get a little too dizzy.

1.If someone were to ask you who Bear Country's busiest creatures are, you might answer that bees are the busiest. They gather nectar and pollen, make honey, guard the hive, and do all the other things that have earned them the title Busy Bees. Or you might answer that beavers are the busiest. They fell trees, make dams, and build lodges with secret underwater entrances. There's no question about it, beavers certainly are busy.

But if you were to answer bees or beavers, you would be wrong. Because the busiest creatures in Bear Country, lately, are none other than our friends the Bear family. The Bears haven't always been so busy. They used to do the things that most families do: they worked and played, went to school, visited friends, enjoyed nature—and once in a while they just sat around and did absolutely nothing.

2. The Bears hadn't planned on becoming so busy—it sort of sneaked up on them. First, there was Brother Bear and the Little League. Then, Sister Bear got bitten by the ballet bug and started ballet class.

When her best friend, Lizzy Bruin, started riding lessons, Sister just *had* to take that up too—and Brother wasn't about to be left out of something as exciting as horseback riding.

3. That's how it was with other activities. As soon as one of the cubs' friends signed up for something, Brother and Sister had to sign up too. Before anyone thought to say enough is enough, they were also signed up for...swimming, gymnastics, soccer, (SOCCER IS HOW WE GET OUR KICKS!) karate, art (I CALL IT "FLOWER WITH DRIPS") and computer club.

4. Talk about busy! Mama or Papa Bear had to *drive* Brother and Sister to all those activities!

Things got so complicated that Mama had to make a big schedule to keep things straight. Papa hung it on the wall.

5. The schedule was especially difficult on Friday—and today was Friday. "Will somebody answer

the phone?" called Mama, after the fourth ring. "I'm busy getting things out of the freezer for tonight's dinner."

"Can't right now!" shouted Sister from upstairs. "I'm getting ready for ballet!"

"Me neither!" yelled Brother. "I'm getting on my baseball stuff!"

6. Since Papa was out working on the car, Mama had to answer the phone. She reached it by the seventh ring. It seemed a lot longer to Gran on the other end. "Hello?" said Mama. "Hello, dear," said Gran. "Is everything all right? You sound a little breathless."

"Just a little," said Mama. "I was in the kitchen getting dinner out of the freezer. The cubs are upstairs getting dressed for ballet and baseball, and Papa—"

But before she could explain about Papa, her shoulder bag got tangled in the phone cord, which pulled the phone down with a clunk. "What happened?" shouted Gran. "There was an awful clunk!"

7. "It was just the phone falling—was there anything special, Gran?" What Mama didn't explain was that when she stooped to pick up the phone, her hat fell off, and when she reached for it, she tripped over the cord and was now sitting in a tangled heap on the floor.

"I was just calling to invite you all to dinner sometime soon," said Gran.

"Love to, Gran. But we're just on our way out, so let me check our schedule and get back to you."

"Fine," Gran said after a pause. "Well, g'bye."

"Mama!" said Sister. "What are you doing sitting on the floor playing with the phone cord? C'mon, we're going to be late!"

"Drop me off first!" shouted Brother on the way to the car. "No! Me first!" cried Sister. "No, me!" insisted Brother.

8. When Papa tried to explain what had been wrong with the car—the spark plugs needed cleaning—Mama shouted, "Not now, dear!" and roared off, leaving him in a cloud of dust.

"Well," Gran said as she hung up the phone, "there certainly is a lot going on over at the tree house."

"That's the way young folks are," said Gramps. "They like to get out and *do* things. Why, when I was a young feller—"

"*Doing* is one thing," said Gran. "*Over*doing," she added with a sigh, "is something else again." If Papa could have heard Gran, he surely would have agreed. There was too much going on—too much coming and going, too much rushing about, *too much pressure*. The Bear family's schedule was becoming a nightmare—as it turned out, a whole series of nightmares. The cubs had planned to watch some TV that evening, but they were so stiff and tired—Sister from ballet, Brother from baseball—that they went to bed early, fell asleep, and dreamed.

9. Sister dreamed she was on a strange sort of merry-go-round—a merry-go-round of activities, which went round and round and round. She wanted to get off, but no matter how hard she tried, she couldn't. Brother had a dream too. He dreamed he was caught up in an enormous whirlwind of baseballs, soccer balls, and computers.

Papa dreamed he was trapped on a magic carpet that was zooming into a deep black hole. Only it wasn't a magic carpet. It was that awful schedule from the wall. Mama didn't have a nightmare. The reason was that she didn't fall asleep all night. She lay awake staring into the darkness, wondering how she was going to get through the next day.

10. After a quick breakfast, Mama packed a lunch for Papa, who headed for some work in the forest. Then she shooed the cubs into the car. "Hurry!" she said. "We have a difficult day ahead of us. There's art class, soccer, karate, and swimming, and we've got to squeeze in lunch and shopping!"

They climbed into the car, and she turned the key. But the engine wouldn't start. She tried again, but it still wouldn't start.

"Please, Mama!" shouted Brother. "Our karate instructor is very strict about being late!"

"And the soccer coach is worse!" yelled Sister. Mama tried again and again.

"Please, Mama!" they screamed, jumping up and down in the back seat. But no matter how hard she tried, the car just would not start.

11. Then Mama did something the cubs had never seen her do before. She started to cry. Big wet tears rolled down her cheeks. The cubs forgot karate and soccer and everything else except that their

mama was crying. “What’s the matter?” asked Brother.

“Tell us, *please!*” begged Sister. But Mama just went boohooing up the front steps and into the house. “Go get Papa!” Sister said to Brother. “I’ll stay with Mama.”

Sister followed Mama up to her room, where she fell on the bed sobbing. It was all Sister could do to keep from crying herself.

12. “It’s Mama! You gotta come!” shouted Brother as he reached Papa’s workplace in the woods. He told Papa what happened. Papa could see that he was upset about Mama crying.

“Everybody cries once in a while, Son,” he said. “Even you?” asked Brother.

“Sometimes,” Papa said. “The problem with the car is those spark plugs. We probably need new ones. But the real problem is this schedule of ours. I know Mama didn’t sleep well last night worrying about it.” “I didn’t sleep too well, either. I had this awful dream,” admitted Brother.

“That makes two of us,” said Papa.

“Sister had one too,” said Brother as they reached the tree house.

13. “Mama stopped crying!” announced Sister as Papa and Brother came upstairs. “That’s right,” Mama said, smiling through a few last tears. “There’s nothing like a good cry sometimes.”

“And there’s nothing like a little common sence about too much pressure,” said Papa.

14.So the bears had a family meeting right then and there. The cubs agreed that two after-school activities a week were more than enough. Brother chose baseball and computer club. Sister chose ballet and horseback riding.

True—they lost their title The Busiest Family in Bear Country. But they went back to having a very good time doing the everyday things that most families do. They worked and played, went to school, visited friends, enjoyed nature—

15. and once in a while, they sat around doing absolutely nothing.

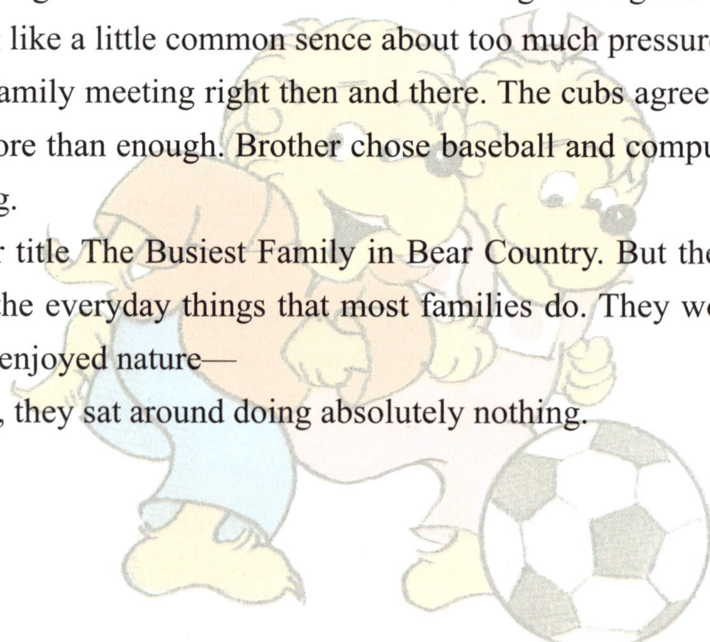